BEDFOR~
Then and Now

Eric G. Meadows

S.B. Publications

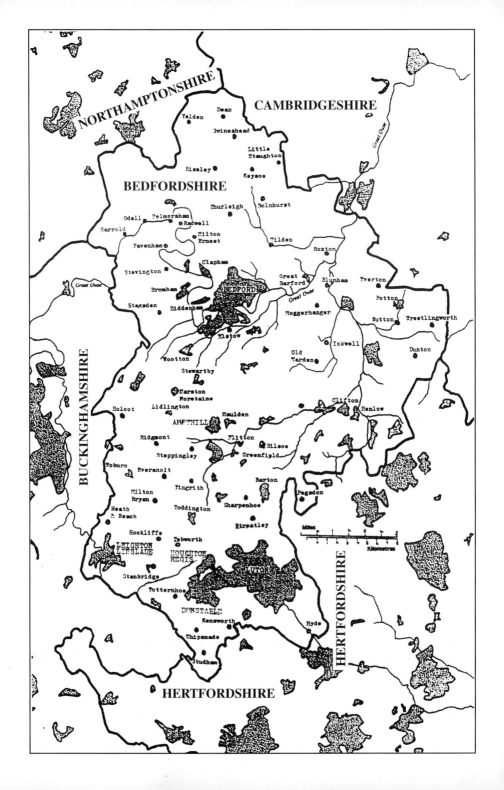

Contents

Front Cover

HOUGHTON REGIS: The middle of the large village, High Street looking west with the house of Tithe Farm on the right, the lock-up on the end of Workhouse Row cottages beyond the two yews, and a former fire station building made into a bus shelter. Half the village buildings were about to be demolished, while the population increased from a little over 3,000 to over 16,000 in 1981. London "overspill" was moved to the new sprawling Tithe Farm estate in 1960-63 and Parkside estate from 1971, both on greenfield sites. Tithe Farm with its great aisled Tithe Barn of about 1400 was torn down to build the two-tiered Bedford Square shopping centre, its crude back facing a wider High Street. The site of Workhouse Row is used for car parking in front of the medieval church, which recently had the Totternhoe stone (clunch) of its 15th century tower restored, and whitewashed for protection. The planners should have given this town a new centre initially, and left the middle of the village as a quiet backwater, as throughout Stevenage New Town; instead it is a chaotic sprawl of suburbia attached to the west of Luton as well as Dunstable.

10th January 1960 and 19th March 1995

ICKWELL: A pair of early 19th century Manor Cottages and an earlier one, backed by horse chestnut, ash and beech in the park of Ickwell Bury. Right-hand one of the pair was home of William Wagstaff, lifelong bellringer. The cottagers shared the essential vegetable garden. Now the pair as a single dwelling has an extension, and the older cottage has been rebuilt as a house, but note the seclusion and modern ideas of a labour-saving garden.

5th October 1958 and 31st May 1995

Introduction

Bedfordshire may seem an ordinary lowland county, but it has great variety of landscape in its small area: downs rise at its south end, an undulating gault-clay vale is followed by the greensand ridge across its middle, then the Great Ouse meanders over the Oxford clay plain; finally there are gentle northern uplands. These are the natural, physical and geological divisions.

For building: flint and hard chalk (clunch) were used in the south, rust-brown sandstone or ironstone from the greensand, cream-grey limestones exposed by the river in the north-west, and timber with plaster mostly on the north uplands. Brickearths in the clays which form the soils of most of the county were used for local bricks, of all shades of red, yellow, purple-grey and blue; apart from a small brickworks at Arlesey using gault clay, only Fletton bricks are made now from the Oxford clay.

The M1 motorway, A5, A6, A1(M) and two main railways cross the county northwards and several more-tortuous roads traverse from east to west. The main towns are on these lines of communication. Luton, Dunstable and Houghton Regis are joined in a sprawling ill-planned conurbation of some 225,000 people, while Bedford/Kempston form a smaller suburbia of 91,000 residents. Between these urban areas are the towns of Leighton Linslade, Ampthill and Flitwick, Sandy and Biggleswade. Most of the villages centre on the nearest town. As part of prosperous south-east England, the 1951 county population of 319,000 in 87,235 dwellings had risen by 1991 to 524,000 in 210,158 dwellings, and the County Council is obliged to plan for estimated further growth.

Road transport has expanded enormously since the M1 opened in 1959, and now conveys most of the freight formerly on railways. This and the stupendous increase in numbers of motor cars has necessitated road widening, construction of bypasses and some new roads. Every road is very busy with continual journeyings between towns, and between town and village.

Far fewer people work on the land due to mechanisation. The automobile has allowed people to live almost anywhere, so villages are now full of townspeople. The newcomers frequently do not know, understand or want to understand country ways of life. Their urban ideas are reflected in the alterations to the house or cottage that is their home. Few have in their gardens the fine displays of flowers which were once common, or grow crops of vegetables and fruit. Spaces within villages are often infilled, sometimes with poor imitation styles or houses totally out of keeping with their neighbours. Groups or estates of nearly identical housing of inferior design are added by developers; as a result some villages seem congested, uniform and like suburban outliers. Thatch gives variety and individuality. Shops in smaller villages may have gone completely or been reduced to a post office/store. Bus services into town may be non-existent or minimal, making life difficult for anyone without a car.

The countryside has always been fully farmed, with small areas of wood; arable predominates and more so with intensification. Market gardening on sand or gravel in the Flitt, Ivel or lower Ouse valleys has tended to decline and employment in forestry is very small. Water meadows by the Great Ouse have been drained and ploughed, but any surviving old pasture will almost certainly have been "improved". The oldest grassland is on the rural downs, part of the Chilterns Area of Outstanding Natural Beauty, but lack of grazing by sheep and rabbits has allowed hawthorn scrub to replace much of it. Hedgerow trees are less numerous, almost all elms died from Dutch elm disease in the 1970s and other trees went when hedges were destroyed; remaining hedges are often abandoned to tall growth, are stunted remnants or trimmed with flail-cutters. Some of the best countryside is in country parks, nature reserves, and properties of the National Trust or the Woodland Trust.

In the following illustrations few of the current pictures show an improvement on the earlier subject or scene. Sometimes changes are slight, but in others they are amazing!

Downland

HYDE: Trains on the London Midland railway crossing the county boundary. Diesel units replaced the steam locomotives generally in the 1960s, later the line was electrified. Cooters End Lane here is the county boundary, looking north over East Hyde to barren arable land of the Luton Hoo Estate. *21st December 1957 and 17th February 1995*

HYDE: Watercress beds fed by a spring, and vegetable plots, by the River Lea. The beds continued beyond the road towards early 19th century Hyde Mill, on the site of a Domesday watermill. The trees on the background slope are in parkland of a Georgian house, *The Hyde*, changed to arable farmland now. The beds were probably abandoned because flow of the spring became unreliable, but it is a pity the foreground is derelict.

24th April 1955 and 18th February 1995

LUTON: Early Victorian houses in Church Street faced a large, once pollarded, English elm which shows this was formerly a country churchyard. The tree died in the mid 1970s from Dutch elm disease. The Arndale Centre, containing market hall, shops, and car parks, was built 1969-77 and was being refurbished in 1995.

23rd February 1963 and 2nd March 1995

LUTON: The main street, George Street looking north-west to the 1934-8 Town Hall, with ABC cinema and the little dome on Blundell's clothing shop. People sit by a flower bed on the Corn Exchange site and the blue-painted police telephone post was being replaced by a paler one. Before 1995 the street was partly pedestrianised, with trees in place of the flower bed and Barclays Bank rebuilt as part of the Arndale development.

23rd May 1962 and 16th February 1995

LUTON: Stuart Street at the Wellington Street crossing looking to the 1865-6 King Street Congregational church of Kentish rag and the 1851-2 Methodist chapel, just as the south side of the street was being demolished to make part of the Inner Ring Road. The new road was needed for east-west traffic to bypass the Victorian centre of the town. Office blocks of red-brick now stand on the church sites.

25th July 1967 and 16th February 1995

LUTON: Old and new industries: a mid-Victorian house and manufactory in Melson Street torn down for an Arndale Centre car park; a stone's throw away in widened Church Street and seen from the car park are new factories of yellow and red brick.

22nd March 1960 and 1st July 1974

LUTON: Moat House at Biscot, a medieval hall dating from about 1380 with its moat intact, when it was a farmhouse and open country stretched northwards to the downs near Warden Hill. In 1967-8 it was restored as *Old Moat House* pub and restaurant, where one can dine under the moulded and embattled beams and arched braces of the hall roof of about 1500.

11th February 1956 and 16th February 1995

LUTON: From a lynchet on Bradger's Hill looking north-west over fields of Stopsley Common to Warden Hill. The houses are in Fairford Avenue. Now the fields are covered by the Bushmead and other housing estates, retaining the white-walled house of Stopsley Common Farm, but most of the lynchet has a thicket of hawthorns. A black speck against the sky, the central beech is seen again on the next page.

24th July 1958 and 2nd February 1995

LUTON: From the lower slopes of Warden Hill looking south-west towards Limbury and Leagrave. A white cloud in the centre may be steam from a train near Leagrave station. Closer are a few dwellings along Birdsfoot Lane. On the right are houses around *The Warden Tavern*, then a separate development in the parish of Streatley. The recent view shows tower blocks of flats at Hockwell Ring and on Marsh Farm estate.

6th February 1947 and 20th January 1995

STUDHAM: On high ground in the far south of the county, this view is from a footpath just beyond the church looking north to a considerable housing estate at Holywell that has developed in the last fifty years. The ash trees remain in the hedge but the pasture is now arable.

4th March 1956 and 26th February 1995

WHIPSNADE: A 16th or 17th century house, with golden leaves on the large elm beside it, at the east end of the long undulating green, when the house was *Anne's Café.* Now, very much enlarged, it is *Old Hunter's Lodge,* with the dead elm trunk used as support for a name board.

9th November 1958 and 26th February 1995

KENSWORTH: In a pleasantly secluded and wooded valley at Kensworth Lynch, east of the village, are Corner Farm and some 17-18th century timber-framed houses. Additions and alterations to these buildings and their grounds have been considerable.

27th September 1958 and 22nd March 1990

DUNSTABLE: *The White Horse* was a timber-framed Tudor inn with coach entrance to stables at the rear. It had decorated oak beams inside and was refronted with brick in the 18th century. It stood on the north side of Church Street and was demolished to make the street a dual carriageway when a new shopping mall was built in the mid-1960s.

7th May 1960 and 21st March 1995

DUNSTABLE: Part of Dunstable Downs, highest ground in the county, seen from the road to Tring. The hill on the left is Five Knolls which has seven bronze age barrows on its top. Because of rising currents of air over these slopes, the London Gliding Club has the next field to the west. Over the years hawthorn scrub has increased but trees on the left are in gardens.

2nd November 1957 and 8th April 1995

TOTTERNHOE: English elms were abundant west of the Knolls until killed by Dutch elm disease. Here are tall ones by a buttercup-filled pasture on Manor Farm looking north-west to the little hill at Billington. The last of a haystack stands near the barns. By 1995 elm suckers beside the road had made small trees, but the only large trees in the open landscape were willows. An electric fence divided the pony grazing of sown grass.

June 1945 and 8th April 1995

TODDINGTON: (OS 166: TL 011314). At the north end of the parish on a footpath going east just beyond Long Lane Farm, looking south-east to the downs from Sharpenhoe Clappers (left) to Sundon limeworks pit (right). The little fields and pastures divided by hedges with trees were typical of mixed farming on the clay, a year before construction of the M1 motorway began; part of Redhills Farm glimpsed in the centre and many elms near Old Park (right). Intensive mechanised farming has caused most of the visual change, but the motorway produces continuous noise intrusion with much atmospheric pollution.

22nd September 1957 and 20th April 1995

23

STREATLEY: The hill road from the village goes north-west down Moleskin to the hamlet of Sharpenhoe. Beyond is a patchwork of fields and trees at Pulloxhill and the horizon is the wooded greensand ridge. Chalk for marling fields was once dug from the wayside. where the grassland has a rich and varied flora, now much decreased due to growth of scrub woodland. The ground right of the road is part of the National Trust property.

21st January 1967 and 20th January 1995

STREATLEY: From the west bank of the road down Moleskin, to the north is the distinctive hill-spur, The Clappers, capped by a beech grove and given in 1939 to the National Trust. Hawthorn growth compelled a slightly lower viewpoint, but increase of trees and bushes with loss of grassland is obvious. The Trust have sheep to graze the upper slopes for part of the year.

21st July 1962 and 22nd July 1995

STREATLEY: Sharpenhoe means 'Steep hill-spur'. These hills, locally called The Clappers, seen from the south-east on the Luton to Barton main road when there was plenty of grassland on their ribbed slopes. The Barton bypass now crosses the foreground and snow shows clearly how dense the woodland has become.

6th October 1946 and 4th March 1995

STREATLEY: Table Hill, most southerly of the eastern spurs of The Clappers, and Smithcombe Hill (right) above Watergutter Hole, with Cow Hole (left) seen from above Barton Cutting on the Luton to Bedford main road. Chalk underlying the land, which included the original viewpoint, was used for the bypass embankments. The County Council now manages this area and has introduced goats experimentally to reduce scrub, patches have been cleared for them (right).

6th October 1946 and 20th January 1995

BARTON IN THE CLAY: On a south summit of the Barton Hills looking north-west to a central little beech hanger, Leete Wood, and to Sharpenhoe Clappers. The Springs are in trees south of the valley's curve. The slopes above them are now lost in scrub woodland, but other slopes are cleared manually and grazed by sheep to maintain the chalk flora in a National Nature Reserve.

2nd March 1947 and 4th March 1995

PEGSDON: The name means 'valley by a peak', for a deep curving coombe with steeper side-valleys is dominated by the rounded east summit of Deacon Hill making lovely downs, the most easterly in the county. Lynchets show near the hilltop. Grazing has been regular, so there are expanses of grassland with flowers in season. Large hawthorns now hide the original view and, at a slightly lower viewpoint, sycamore saplings have grown from seed blown in from Hexton estate.

7th May 1961 and 4th May 1995

Gault and Greensand

SILSOE: 17-18th century timber-framed and plastered houses, with interesting chimney pots, in the High Street when it was the Luton to Bedford main road. The middle house was demolished to build a shop set back from the street, but loss of the house disturbed the balance of the buildings and spoiled their pleasant grouping. The village is now bypassed, but there has been no further change in this part of High Street.

25th April 1954 and 16th April 1974

SILSOE: On the hill near Thrift Wood south-west of the village, the view eastwards is over fields of corn in shocks. So as not to foul the reaper, a low bough was sawn off the ash and left on the unused bridleway. Now large elms have gone but a thicket of elm suckers remains in the centre. Oilseed rape has been harvested from the pale fields, beans grow in the foreground and the sawn bough is still alive!

25th August 1946 and 22nd July 1995

FLITTON: A market gardening village where houses and barns cluster round the fine church of local ironstone, built 1440-89 for the de Grey family of Wrest, with their later mausoleum attached to its east end. Leeks grow on a sandy plot in the foreground, while cedars and other trees stand in grounds of the former rectory. New dwellings and their gardens now occupy the viewpoint.

16th February 1958 and 2nd May 1974

GREENFIELD: A pair of thatched cottages, Nos. 3 and 5 Mill Lane, homes of local market gardeners; they have now been made into a single dwelling, well thatched and without a chimney stack. The mill was a watermill on the River Flitt.

19th June 1960 and 9th July 1995

TINGRITH: A very small village, it has some bargeboarded early Victorian estate houses near the church. This was the Victorian inn, *The Swan,* licensee Mrs. Harris on the doorstep. The building is now a private dwelling, *Old Swan House.*

10th September 1955 and 19th March 1995

MILTON BRYAN: One of the attractive villages of mid-Bedfordshire, the further end of this group of three 16th century houses was the post office and shop. It faces the side of *The Red Lion*, a 17th century timber-framed building with a later brick front including diaperwork and ornate bargeboards. A farm worker carries a milk can on his bicycle. The houses are now well restored as two dwellings.

2nd July 1957 and 30th June 1995

TEBWORTH: Chalgrave National School, opened in 1855 and closed on 22nd July 1983, was built of yellow gault bricks with red-brick dressings. The buildings are now two private dwellings. The early Victorian house on the right, end of a row, has been replaced by semi-detached houses.

20th March 1960 and 16th February 1995

HOCKLIFFE: At Church End on a low hill, a 17th century timber-framed farmhouse with fruit and vegetables in its garden and a Victorian cottage row south of the church. The giant elms have now gone but limes remain in the churchyard and the buildings are well maintained, the house behind a tall hedge.

1st February 1959 and 16th February 1995

STANBRIDGE: The church of ironstone and Totternhoe stone at the north-east end of the small village-green where milk churns awaited collection. By 1995 the telephone pole had gone but there were more overhead electricity cables, a path with kerbs by the green, more houses in the distance and few large trees.

2nd October 1955 and 26th February 1995

LEIGHTON BUZZARD: The impressive early 15th century Market Cross at the end of High Street shows for how long this town has been an important trading place. The 16-19th century buildings near it have been modified quite a lot in a short time and perhaps made more like a stage set. The market is now held in an open area behind the buildings on south side of the street.
21st February 1960 and 26th February 1995

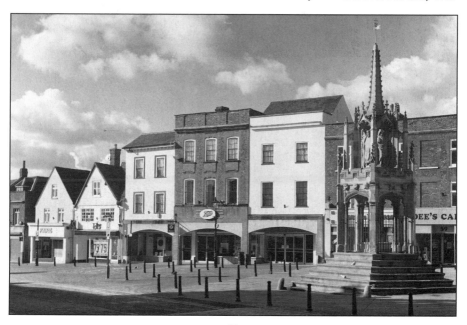

LINSLADE: Commercial barges on the Grand Union Canal passing *The Globe,* the small pub in flat pastures lined by pollarded willows between canal and river Ouzel. Now narrowboats for pleasure are moored here, the willows have just been left to grow and the larger pub seems to be Mecca for thirsty motorists.

21st February 1960 and 26th February 1995

HEATH AND REACH: Heathland with heather and gorse is now quite rare on the greensand. This was Shire Heath when it had gorse, young birches and scattered old pines. Most of it was made into pine plantations but a small southern portion, which was left open, has been degraded by bracken, birches and lack of grazing or cutting.

20th May 1962 and 21st March 1995

WOBURN has some of the finest Georgian buildings in the county. In High Street are three-storey houses and shops of the 1740s which have rubbed-brick arches and carved keystones over segment-headed windows with aprons, also giant pilasters. Red and dark-glazed local bricks give richness and pattern to the walls. Two shops have delicate windows, a grocers' and an ironmongers' with petrol pump. Now the shops sell antiques, china and gifts or are restaurants.

23 May 1959 and 20th April 1995

HOLCOT or HULCOTE: This beautiful church, smallest of six in England built in the reign of Elizabeth I, was 'reedified .. at his owne proper charge' (inscribed on the family monument) 1590-93 by Richard Chernocke, lord of the manor. The ancient lime avenue (right) led to his mansion, demolished in the early 19th century. The spreading wych-elm and English elms died in the mid-1970s and only sown rye-grass grows in the field.

12th September 1954 and 22nd June 1995

EVERSHOLT is in lovely wooded but farmed countryside of the ducal estate, its buildings scattered in fourteen 'ends' linked by lanes. Here is the road from Tyrell's End going west to Hill's End and Froxfield when it was lined by great English elms grown up from the hedge. There are still elm suckers in the hedge.

13th October 1956 and 19th March 1995

EVERSHOLT: Witts End Close, a 16th or 17th century timber-framed farmhouse which had been converted into two cottages and was semi-derelict, but was admirably restored about thirty years ago. The flowers in the foreground are in the garden of the next cottage. The winch for drawing water is a genuine one on the well-head.

30th September 1956 and 19th March 1995

STEPPINGLEY: Steppingley church, rebuilt 1859-60, was the first of several churches in the county planned for the Duke of Bedford by architect Henry Clutton. About 1870 he designed the school and schoolhouse, both using local ironstone in a Tudor style, seen here with a 16-17th century timber-framed cottage. The school is now *The Folly,* a private house, and an extension has just been made to the far side of the cottage.

30th September 1956 and 9th May 1995

RIDGMONT: A pair of cottages with most colourful gardens, but missing the front railings which were taken for scrap iron in a 1940 war effort (but never used). The cobbler's business for the village was also here. In 1985-6 the building was restored, the rendering removed to expose the 16th century timber-frame, to which an upper storey was added in the 17th or 18th century.

20th September 1953 and 21st March 1995

LIDLINGTON: The older part of this village is situated on the steep north side of the greensand ridge looking over Marston Vale. The central thatched building was the village hall, converted from timber-framed cottages, its rounded thatch similar to the roof on the timber-framed *Green Man*. The village hall has been replaced and *The Red Lion* is now a pair of houses.

28th August 1960 and 15th May 1995

AMPTHILL: In the compact centre of the little country town, this was looking east in Woburn Street outside *The Queen's Head.* Many details of the buildings have changed and *The George* has become a private house; also the signs, street furniture and means of transport are different. Sandhill House on the left has a much poorer garden.

27th June 1954 and 22nd June 1995

AMPTHILL: Church Street begins at the market place where a wooden arcaded Georgian shop was a butchers'. It faces a Georgian house with a beautiful shop window and the whitened Georgian front of the former *King's Arms,* a 17th century coaching inn. A small 17th century house has been replaced by a three-storey building with an entry to Printer's Court behind it. The arcaded shop, which sells china, faces an antiques shop and bridal boutique.

8th September 1957 and 9th July 1995

MAULDEN: Water End is situated by the River Flitt where there was a watermill at Mill Farm. Here on the side of a lane stood a pair of 17-18th century cottages, home of farm workers, with a vehicle entry and ironstone wall by the field at the further end. The cottages now form one large dwelling, outside which a gnome gazes over an extensive grassy paddock.

September 1942 and 9th May 1995

OLD WARDEN: Among low wooded hills, this estate village was made fashionably picturesque about 1830-60 by the 3rd Lord Ongley; from 1871 added to and well maintained by the Shuttleworth family. No. 28 is typical *cottage orné*. It is timber-framed and plastered, perhaps 18th century, with the chimney, thatch and ridge tiles altered in mid-19th century. A house built about 1978 is set behind conifers and bushes, so the view of more distant cottages has been lost.

11th September 1973 and 23rd June 1995

OLD WARDEN: There is space south-west of No. 28 to No. 32, but their gardens are no longer crammed with flowers, fruit and vegetables as when they were the homes of estate or farm workers. Both cottages had their walls pale ochre washed but are now ivory or white. There used to be a plum tree by the road next to No. 28. These cottages are ideally sited, with others facing them on the bank above the village street.

5th October 1958 and 29th July 1995

ICKWELL: A hamlet of Northill, is mostly built around a spacious green with parkland of The Bury west of it. There are timber-framed or brick cottages of 17-19th centuries, some over-restored, also more recent houses. The permanent maypole is used by the local children each May, now usually on the May Bank Holiday. At other seasons village football or cricket can be seen here, where centrepiece of the green is an immense oak.

18th May 1957 and 6th March 1983

CLIFTON: Grange Street, a twisting street with old buildings at different angles to it, and the Coronation Garden planted in 1953 by the village pond. One can see changed signs, lamps and road markings, a bungalow in place of a barn, more parked cars and how much the weeping willow has grown.

19th July 1959 and 18th March 1995

HENLOW: High Street has attractively varied houses of local yellow and red brick, some fronting directly on to the pavement, others behind garden walls, built during the last three centuries. A new shop has opened but *The Parachute* pub, named for airmen from RAF Henlow Camp, seems to have moved or gone. Slight curves in the otherwise straight street complete a comfortable feeling of enclosure.

12th October 1958 and 23rd February 1995

DUNTON: *The Bell,* a charming little pub which sold Simpsons Baldock ales and stood on the end of a Victorian cottage-row in Millow beside the road from the south. The many elms and large ash have died, and the cottages have been replaced by bungalows further from the road, the garage of one of them showing over the hedge.

12th October 1958 and 31st May 1995

WRESTLINGWORTH: The most easterly village in the county, near the Cambridgeshire border. *The Chequers* was a small 17th century pub fronting straight on to a busy road. Now much enlarged, it is still an attractive feature in the village street. The house on the road-bend was extended and hides behind cypresses, but a large horse chestnut is still there.

12th October 1958 and 31st May 1995

SUTTON: The Burgoyne family held the manor from about 1500, acquired monastic lands and lived at Sutton Park until 1938. Many dwellings in this small village are estate houses or timber-framed cottages, such as this early 19th century Gothic one with great horse chestnuts behind it. Spaces between the older houses have been filled recently.

5th April 1974 and 18th March 1995

POTTON is an attractive old market town in the market gardening area, now home for commuters. On its south edge, where the Biggleswade and Sandy roads meet, is *The Royal Oak* and a thatched cottage, both timber-framed and plastered buildings. The 700-foot television mast on Sandy Heath shows in the background. Telephone wires have multiplied.

16th August 1959 and 18th March 1995

EVERTON stands on the east end of the greensand ridge which crosses the county from the south-west. Its light soil is ideal for market gardening and was growing runner beans and other vegetables in 1958. The church tower was struck by lightning in 1974, and restored without the belfry but with pinnacles. New houses have been erected near the church and ugly barns behind them.

12th October 1958 and 18th March 1995

ROXTON: A group of thatched cottages in High Street, perhaps early 19th century, built for the Metcalfe estate which converted a barn into a picturesque chapel with rustic verandah and thatch in 1824. Late Victorian-style cast-iron standpipes, made by Glenfield & Kennedy of Kilmarnock, were installed in the 1930s in many north Bedfordshire villages. This one has a spanner key to operate it, water coming from the lion's mouth into a pail.

11th April 1954 and 23rd June 1995

BLUNHAM: The middle of the small village with its enjoyable medley of old buildings when this was a quiet bend in High Street. Above *The Horseshoes* rises the ironstone pinnacled top, late Gothic work dated 1583, of the church's west tower seen in evening light. The pantiled dwellings and earlier one end-on to the street have gone, leaving two thatched cottages dated 1666 and 1699.

22nd May 1961 and 22nd June 1995

MOGGERHANGER: A little village with thatched cottages at the central crossing of the Bedford to Sandy main road, seen here from St. John's Road with a barn, yew and old house of Village Farm. Now there are new houses and street lamps at the crossing where only the further thatched cottage remains. The pyramidal roof is on the chancel tower of the 1860-61 church designed by William Slater. Park House, by Soane 1809, is now being restored.

5th October 1958 and 18th March 1995

GREAT BARFORD: The beautiful and justly popular view, from the south-west (Blunham) bank, of the gabled 16th century house of Bridge Farm, the church, the white-walled *Anchor Inn* and part of the old bridge; a view which is sadly changed. The river was dredged for navigation in 1975-6, but the main change is due to growth of Lombardy poplars, cypresses and willows.

3rd July 1960 and 23rd June 1995

BEDFORD: The urban tree-lined river east to County Hall 1968-9, its lower wing and part of Mander College seen over the cast-iron 1883-4 Prebend Street Bridge. County Bridge was opened in 1992. The lower wing, which houses the County Record Office, is still there but is now mostly hidden by willows.

24th October 1971 and 9th July 1995

ELSTOW: Medieval houses in High Street when they were mostly covered with pebble dash and owned by the Whitbread family, who sold them in 1974 for £1 to the Borough Council of Bedford, which restored them in 1976. The arch over the entrance to a coaching inn and the curved braces may be 14th century work.

8th May 1960 and 9th September 1977

ELSTOW: The late 15th or early 16th century Moot Hall, jettied all round, with upper meeting room over eight individual shops, was nearly derelict in 1950 when the owners, the Whitbread family, gave it to the village. Original doorways and windows of the shops were bricked up. It was restored by the County Council in 1951 and now has a permanent exhibition of 17th century life and associations with John Bunyan.

September 1942 and 9th May 1995

MARSTON MORETAINE: This Saxon 'marshy place' is in the vale blighted, like the village, by expediencies of the Fletton brick industry. However its church is a jewel comparable in grandeur with Norfolk churches. It resembles Elstow in having a massive detached tower, the belfry about 1340 as are the chancel and vestry of dark ironstone. The tall nave with aisles was rebuilt 1445-50. This splendid grouping from the north-west is now lost. The view from the north shows house rows allowed by planners with no regard for the surroundings, also a 10-15 foot hawthorn hedge.

1st November 1958 and 9th May 1995

STEWARTBY: The Fletton brickworks of London Brick Company in 1936 was the largest brickworks in the world. It uses the grey-green shale-like deposit in the Oxford clay, dug by giant electrically-powered dragline excavators and conveyed by belts. The top spoil has been dumped in the bottom of the quarry. Now the works is only a quarter of its former size and coltsfoot is the prime coloniser in this partly reclaimed quarry.

24th August 1969 and 9th July 1995

WOOTTON: At Keeley Green, this is the start of Keeley Lane with *The Rose and Crown* on the bend. It was a charming rural scene so near to Kempston and Bedford. The whole place is now suffering from pressures brought by the motor car, which include an extensive parking area behind the pub for cars of the masses, and large conveniences attached to the building.

5th September 1954 and 22nd September 1993

BIDDENHAM: A timber-framed and brick dovecote of about 1700 by the pond of Manor Farm. Larger breeds than our wild pigeons and doves were reared in these dovecotes, as gifts and to supplement their owners' diet when meat was scarce. The stone wall and dovecote were demolished in 1966, later the farmhouse was changed to a private hospital but the pond, now called Village Pond, has been restored for nature study by schools.

4th August 1957 and 6th March 1995

BROMHAM Mill seen from the long medieval stone bridge over the river and water meadows. The first view shows the mill of stone and brick when it belonged to a farm. The mill's oldest parts, constructed in 1695 and 1722, are nearest the river; the rest of 1858. Originally powered by two wooden undershot waterwheels, a single iron breast wheel of 1908 operates the restored mill. The County Council now owns it and organises exhibitions.

20th April 1958 and 6th March 1995

STAGSDEN: Most southerly of the Bedfordshire villages which use local limestone for cottage and garden walls. A good number of buildings are thatched too, so an attractive place. It was on the main road from Bedford to Newport Pagnell and Milton Keynes, but in 1993 was bypassed. A boy is carrying bottles of milk from the village shop.

16th August 1958 and 29th March 1995

STEVINGTON: The middle of this beautiful limestone village, looking west, retains the late 14th century village cross restored in the 19th century, one of John Bunyan's preaching places. The building on the left was the shop and post office, advertising 'Spillers Shapes for all dogs', 'Lyons tea' and 'Senior Service satisfy'. Now it is only a house, like the off-licence which has had rendering removed. The bunting was for 'VE+50 Day' celebrations.

4th August 1957 and 9th May 1995

HARROLD: There was a minor priory here from 1140, a bridge before 1278 and a market. The small church looks mostly 13th century inside, lofty and light but rather rough. The glory of the church is its west steeple, the tower about 1340 including a west window with flowing tracery, topped about 1500 by a recessed octagonal spire having three tiers of lucarnes and flying buttresses springing from slender corner pinnacles. This is masterly work by Northamptonshire masons using stone from that county, perhaps paid for by the Grey family

of Wrest (Silsoe), lords of the manor. The spire is more sophisticated than the similar one at neighbouring Sharnbrook and excels the 14th century broach spire of Chellington on the opposite hilltop. The pinnacled steeple is a noble sight soaring above roofs and trees in the open shallow valley; here it is seen from the north-west, where a wall and outbuildings of local stone remain.

7th August 1961 and 29th March 1995

PAVENHAM: A stone village where one may feel there has not been much change. Here in the middle, looking east from near the top of Mill Lane, is a cottage group where the total change is considerable: new bay window, doorways gone, an extra window added, a wing rebuilt larger and a great extension behind it. A new house is close on the south side.

20th April 1958 and 29th March 1995

MILTON ERNEST: The village centre is the sloping green with the church at its top among great trees, just east of the main road. Along the south side was the distinctive row of Turnor almshouses built in 1695, replaced in the 1960s by a bold but plain functional row which has the weathered *DONA DEI DEO* stone from the old building set in its central gable. Note the many lovely and characteristic details that might have been conserved.

4th August 1957 and 22nd June 1995

FELMERSHAM: The late 15th century Tithe Barn standing empty after all stock and animals had been sold, its fate unsure. Despite this being a Conservation Area, the planners allowed indifferent, tile-hung urban housing to be squeezed into the farmyard close to the barn by 1972. In 1980 the barn was successfully restored as three two-storey dwellings. My only possible viewpoint for comparison was across the road opposite the handsome bus shelter.

24th October 1970 and 29th March 1995

RADWELL: A large hamlet of Felmersham, this was a pretty place with apple-trees in blossom, neatly trimmed hedges, flowers and young leaves on sycamores, and cow-parsley on the road verge looking north along the lane to Moor End. Now the place has been infilled, and the houses altered by people with different ways of living.

8th May 1960 and 29th March 1995

ODELL: The present Odell Castle was built of stone in 1962 on the site of a Norman motte above the river. Castle and church both stand on knolls among great trees with the road winding in the hollow between them. When the church was entirely rebuilt in the 15th century, as a contrast to spires of neighbouring churches a magnificent west tower was chosen which has clasping buttresses, crenellations and pinnacles. It is reminiscent of Aldwincle and Titchmarsh,

for the stone and masons probably came from that part of Northamptonshire. Recently many of the great horse chestnuts became over-mature, so have been felled or pollarded. Around the west tower a semicircle of evergreens was planted, which has now grown to hide much of the church and mar the view of it; this is nonsensical churchyard gardening.

4th August 1957 and 29th March 1995

CLAPHAM: On the north bank of the river and dominating this main-road village is the tall and strong tower of the church, a sheer 60 feet of Saxon cemented rubble with tiny double-splayed windows, topped by 25 feet of early-Norman belfry. This bold Saxon tower may be the oldest building in the county, probably later 10th century. A triangular-headed doorway into the first floor suggests it was originally a refuge and lookout against Danes, who did come down the Ouse in 1009-10. The buttercupped and daisied orchard is now the playground of Ursula Taylor Lower School.

5th May 1957 and 6th March 1995

THURLEIGH: Here is undulating hill country of glacial boulder clay on Oxford clay, so cultivation would never have been easy. This view northwards is on the rising, falling and twisting lane through Scald End, where the many elms have gone but ashes are growing quickly in a number of the hedges.

22 September 1968 and 15th May 1995

WILDEN: This small, somewhat remote village lies in the little valley of the South Brook. A central grass square has the pub and school by it and, south of the stream, this 16th century house with jettied end and thatched cottages. The church is simple but stately, mostly 15th century and without aisles. Conifers now line part of the stream's bank, so from the white-railed footbridge one sees more of the church, which has lost its turret.

5th August 1957 and 23rd February 1995

BOLNHURST: By the Bedford to Kimbolton road, *Ye Olde Plough* was once the 15th century farmhouse of Brayes, one of a number of medieval enclosed farms here (the open fields were only in the east of the parish). The timber-framed structure had wattle and daub infill, plastered and colour-washed. In 1989 there was a bad fire, but much of the original frame was re-used in the restoration and extensive rebuilding.

9th May 1965 and 15th May 1995

LITTLE STAUGHTON: About half of this village was sacrificed for a Second World War aerodrome. At Green End *The Crown* was a small and charming inn, buttercups and daisies in the grass before it. There are now many new houses in the village, so the inn has been rebuilt to cater for its changed customers and passing trade.

5th August 1957 and 22nd June 1995

KEYSOE: At Hatch End, where the road from Keysoe Row branches north to the isolated church with its landmark spire, stand these little thatched cottages, with pantiles or corrugated iron on roofs of barns and outbuildings. These much-changed former homes of farm labourers reflect the different life styles of their present owners. The background poplars were planted by a farmer to increase trees on the open bleak plateau.

13th September 1958 and 22nd June 1995

RISELEY: Bricks and tiles were made in the village from 1558 until 1894. Here are Nos. 12 (right), 14,16, 18 and 20 High Street. The larger No. 16 is a 16th century timber-framed house end-on to the street, No. 18 is 17th century, the rest early Victorian of red and yellow mottled brick. The garden wall is of a different local brick. No. 18 is now combined with its neighbour and new houses stand to the right.

5th August 1957 and 22nd June 1995

RISELEY: *The Fox and Hounds* is a timber-framed building with lath and plaster walls, probably 16th century, with a Georgian gabled brick addition on the right. It was originally a farmhouse. Quite a lot has changed since its days as a village pub in order to cater for its mobile customers.

13th September 1958 and 22nd June 1995

SWINESHEAD: One of the smallest villages, it had great variety among its lovely old buildings. Typical was this 17-18th century timber-framed house, the plaster honey-coloured, thatch over tiles; thatch also on the further cottage next to the churchyard. The west tower of the church is 14th century with a fine 15th century belfry and spire. Cables and poles have now gone, the cottage has a gabled roof and all the walls are whitened.

11th October 1958 and 6th March 1995

DEAN: From the bridge over the River Til in Lower Dean, children chase after their dad as he goes to tend animals. The Victorian houses have slate roofs but local pantiles are used on outbuildings. Smart detached red-brick houses with dark brown hardwood windows are now to the left behind the horse chestnut and the pub is a private house.

11th October 1958 and 6th March 1995

DEAN: This is a village where the houses and cottages straggle along narrow lanes among trees. *Brookside* was a 17th century half-timbered house facing east over a road and stream to the church on the far side of the green. Remains of a brick tower mill stand on Oak Ley Hill across fields to the west. Now on the roadside rises a row of golden *Cupressocyparis* taller than *Brook End,* a larger house.

11th October 1958 and 6th March 1995

YELDEN: The Norman family of de Trailly held Yelden in 1086 and constructed a motte and bailey castle, using local stone for tower walls and foundations; it was a ruin by 1361. This view north-west from the Swineshead road shows the earthworks and, across the Til valley, the 13th century church, enlarged in the 14th century when its tall tower and squat spire were built. The diminished village has had sensitive infilling recently.

29th May 1960 and 15th May 1995

Index

Acknowledgements

The author/photographer wishes to thank for their assistance: Eric Brandreth (ex Harpenden Librarian), Betty Chambers (editor of the Bedfordshire Magazine), the church architect Victor Farrar, David Henden, and Bedfordshire Record Office.

Thanks to the Head of Ursula Taylor Lower School at Clapham and unknown owners of gardens at Dean and Hockliffe for access to take phographs.

Also thanks to St. Albans Photoprint who aided me with the map.

Finally thanks to my wife Muriel for her patient support.